ERSTE 100 WESENTLICHE WÖRTER

Uhr

Schlüssel

Kamm

Teppich

Kinderbett

Tür

Fenster

Töpfchen

Handtuch

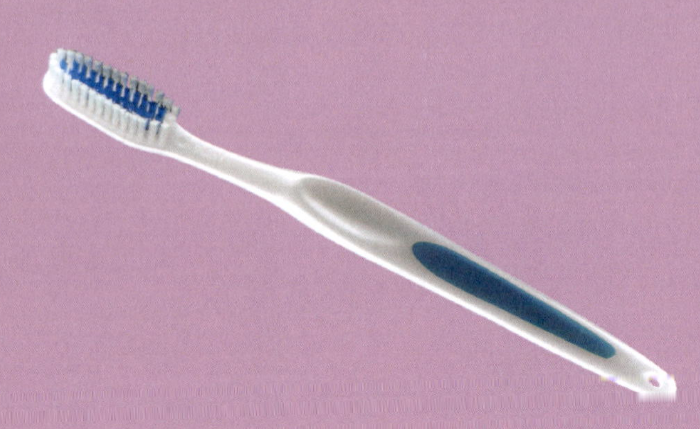

Zahnbürste

Seife

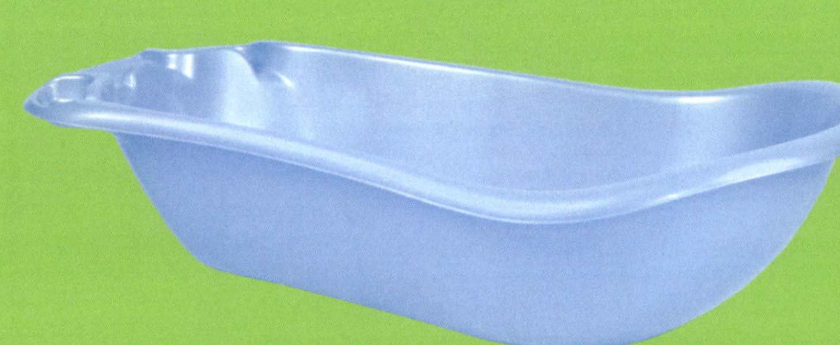

Badewanne

Lätzchen

Eier

Pasta

Suppe

Brot

Käse

Fisch

Saft

Schokolade

Teddybär

Eimer

Formen

Schaufel

Puppe

Buch

Knete

Ball

Wachsmalstifte

Bleistift

Pinsel

Socken

kurze Hose

Hose

Rock

Kleid

Pullover

T-Shirt

Hut

Mütze

Rucksack

Schuhe

Sandalen

Stiefel

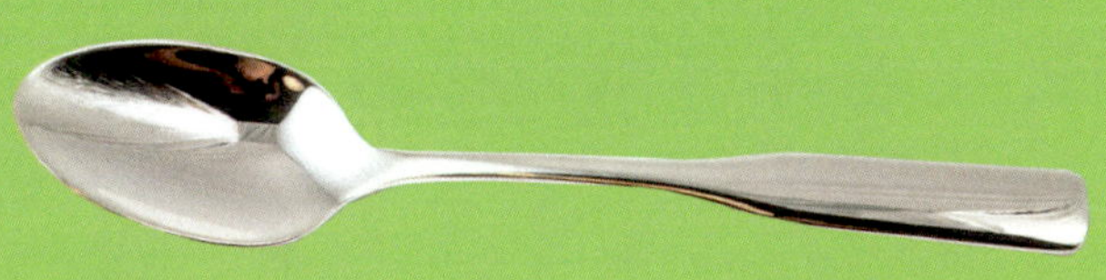

Löffel

Gabel

Tischmesser

Teller

Schüssel

Flasche

Telefon

Kamera

Bügeleisen

Kühlschrank

Tisch

Stuhl

Sessel

Couch

Kinderwagen

Fahrrad

Baum

Auto

Marienkäfer

Blume

Schmetterling

Schiff

Boot

Motorrad

Lastwagen

Zug

Flugzeug

Gurke

Tomate

Kohl

Paprikaschote

Kartoffel

Apfel

Erdbeere

Zitrone

Banane

Birne

Orange

Wassermelone

Melone

Katze

Hund

Schaf

Ziege

Esel

Huhn

Kaninchen

Truthahn

Schwein

Pferd

Kuh

Stier

Ente

Hamster

Papagei

DANKE!

Copyright. All rights Reserved. No part of this publication or the information in it may be quoted from or reproduced in any form by means such as printing, scanning, photocopying or otherwise without prior written permission of the copyright holder. Disclaimer and Terms of Use: Effort has been made to ensure that the information in this book is accurate and complete, however, the author and the publisher do not warrant the accuracy of the information, text and graphics contained within the book due to the rapidly changing nature of science, research, known and unknown facts and internet. The Author and the publisher do not hold any responsibility for errors, omissions or contrary interpretation of the subject matter herein. This book is presented solely for motivational and informational purposes only.

www.ingramcontent.com/pod-product-compliance
Lightning Source LLC
Chambersburg PA
CBRC100835110726
48006CB00009B/1404